anythink

D0602088

FINDING DINOSAURS
VELOCIRAPTOR

by Sheryl Peterson

WWW.FOCUSREADERS.COM

Focus Readers is distributed by North Star Editions:
sales@northstareditions.com | 888-417-0195

Produced for Focus Readers by Red Line Editorial.

Content Consultant: Dr. David B. Weishampel, Professor Emeritus, Center for Functional Anatomy and Evolution, Johns Hopkins University School of Medicine

Photographs ©: Michael Rosskothen/Shutterstock Images, cover, 1; Jakub Czajkowski/ Shutterstock Images, 4–5; Scherl/Sueddeutsche Zeitung Photo/Alamy, 6; Katye Deioma/ ZUMA Press, Inc./Alamy, 9; Photo 12 Collection/Alamy, 11; Elenarts/iStockphoto, 12–13, 20–21, 23; Dirk Wiersma/Science Source, 14; chelsey832/Open Clipart, 16 (human); rikkyal/ iStockphoto, 16 (Velociraptor), 16 (Dilophosaurus), 16 (Tyrannosaurus); UfimtsevaV/ iStockphoto, 16 (Compsognathus), 16 (Allosaurus); wonderlandstock/Alamy, 19; Francois Gohier/Science Source, 25; Adwo/Shutterstock Images, 26–27; Ben Townsend CC 2.0, 29

ISBN
978-1-63517-509-7 (hardcover)
978-1-63517-581-3 (paperback)
978-1-63517-725-1 (ebook pdf)
978-1-63517-653-7 (hosted ebook)

Library of Congress Control Number: 2017948088

Printed in the United States of America
Mankato, MN
November, 2017

ABOUT THE AUTHOR

Sheryl Peterson is the author of many nonfiction books for young readers. She also has an award-winning picture book, *The Best Part of a Sauna*. Sheryl lives near the Canadian border in International Falls, Minnesota. While kayaking in the northern waters, Sheryl has spotted several Velociraptor descendants soaring overhead.

TABLE OF CONTENTS

CHAPTER 1

A SPEEDY THIEF

A strange parade crossed the Gobi Desert in the summer of 1923. Open-topped cars and slow-moving camels made tracks through the sand. The cars carried explorer Roy Chapman Andrews and his team of 40 men from the American Museum of Natural History.

The Bayan Zag region of the Gobi Desert in Mongolia is home to many important fossil finds.

In 1923, Roy Chapman Andrews led the first team to ever discover dinosaur eggs.

The camels carried supplies such as tents, food, and extra cans of gasoline.

It was a risky trip. The sun shone down scorching hot. Swirling winds blew grit into the men's eyes. Snakes and bandits lurked in the hills. But Andrews pushed his team forward. They were on a mission to find buried dinosaur bones.

The caravan frightened the people of China and Mongolia. Many of them had never seen motorcars. Some people called the travelers "dragon hunters" because they believed the fossils in their hills were bones from **prehistoric** dragons.

The expedition set up camp in an area of orange-red cliffs. Andrews had named the spot Flaming Cliffs during his first trip to the region. At sunset, the rocks appeared to be on fire.

Andrews and his team found several Protoceratops bones. They also found a nest of ancient eggs. Near the nest was another discovery. The team uncovered a skull, front claw, and hind foot from a small dinosaur. They found its jaws and finger bones, too. No one had seen this kind of dinosaur before.

After careful study, the new dinosaur was named Velociraptor. The name means "speedy thief" in Latin. Scientists believed the dinosaur lived during the Late Cretaceous period, similar to many other fossils found in the area. But that was all they knew. It took many years of study to learn this mysterious

Dinosaurs!

From the time we first found their
fossils, dinosaurs have captured our
imaginations. Through our expeditions
in the field and our work in the lab, we
continue to make discoveries about
these amazing animals.

Velociraptor mongoliensis was the species that Andrews and his team uncovered.

dinosaur's secrets. There are still only two known **species** of Velociraptor. One is *Velociraptor mongoliensis*. The other is *Velociraptor osmolskae.*

PRESERVING FOSSILS

Uncovering a dinosaur skeleton is a long process. Fossils are buried beneath deep layers of rock. Plus, many fossils are fragile. They can break easily. People must use great care when digging them up.

When Andrews and his team found fossils in the Gobi Desert, they wrapped the fossils in burlap. This rough fabric helped protect the fossils. Team members used paste made from flour and water to hold the burlap together. Soon they had used up all the burlap they brought. So, the team ripped up tent flaps, towels, and clothes to wrap the fossils. One dinosaur skull was even wrapped using striped pajamas.

Scientists also work to preserve the fossils that have already been **excavated**. Fossils or **casts** are

Andrews and his team returned to the Gobi Desert for another expedition in 1928.

often joined together to look like dinosaurs. They are put on display in museums.

CHAPTER 2

SMALL BUT DEADLY

Velociraptor was approximately the size of a turkey. Still, the dinosaur would have been a powerful **predator.** Its jaws held long rows of razor-sharp teeth. The teeth had jagged edges, similar to a saw. Each of Velociraptor's front feet had a large, sharp claw. Its hind feet had curved claws as well.

Velociraptor probably stood on two legs.

13

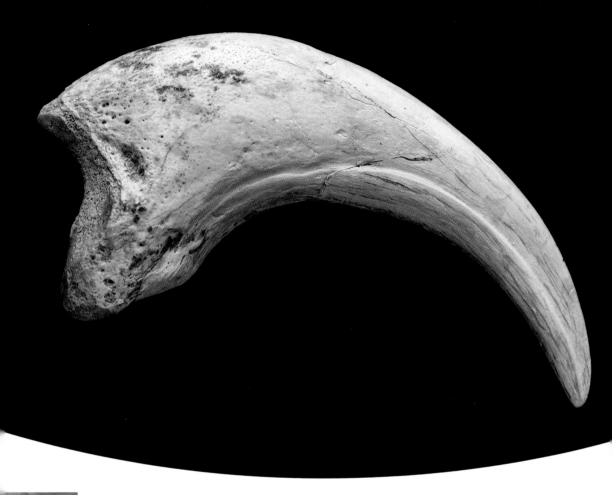

The back claw of a Velociraptor could be 3.5 inches (8.9 cm) long.

Velociraptor's back claws were much like an owl's talons. The claws folded up when the dinosaur ran. It used the claws as hooks when it pounced on its prey. They gripped the prey as Velociraptor ate.

Velociraptor's skull was about the size of a coyote's. Compared with the size of Velociraptor's body, its brain was fairly large. This meant Velociraptor was one of the more intelligent dinosaurs. Many plant-eating dinosaurs had huge bodies and tiny heads. Velociraptor was probably smarter than these dinosaurs. But it was still only about as smart as a pigeon.

Velociraptor had keen eyesight. Scientists analyzed the circles of bone around the dinosaur's eye **sockets**. They learned that its eyes faced forward. Its neck joint allowed the dinosaur to turn its head back and forth quickly. It could have easily seen any movement in the desert.

Plus, Velociraptor could run quickly on its two back feet. It could reach speeds of up to 33 miles per hour (53 km/h). A straight tail made of stiff, hard bone

DINOSAUR DASH

Researchers estimated the speed of Velociraptor and other two-legged dinosaurs compared to a human.

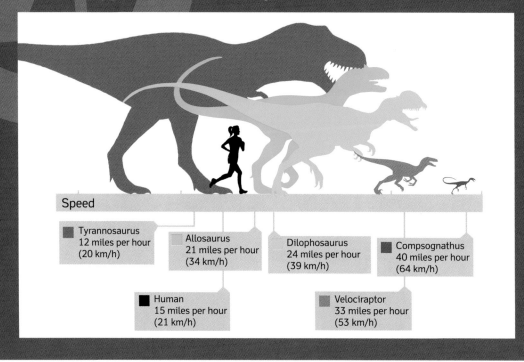

Speed

Tyrannosaurus
12 miles per hour
(20 km/h)

Allosaurus
21 miles per hour
(34 km/h)

Dilophosaurus
24 miles per hour
(39 km/h)

Compsognathus
40 miles per hour
(64 km/h)

Human
15 miles per hour
(21 km/h)

Velociraptor
33 miles per hour
(53 km/h)

helped the dinosaur balance while running.

At first, scientists thought Velociraptor had scales like a reptile. But in 2007, **paleontologists** made a puzzling discovery. They examined a Velociraptor skeleton that had been found in 1998. The skeleton's arm bones had bumps called quill knobs. Birds have these bumps on their bones. For this reason, scientists now believe Velociraptor had feathers. This discovery supported the theory that birds **evolved** from dinosaurs.

Even though Velociraptor had feathers and light bones, it could not fly. Its arms were too short to lift its body weight.

However, flapping its feathered arms might have helped Velociraptor to jump higher when chasing prey. Or, the dinosaur might have flapped its arms to run faster up steep sand dunes.

In addition, the feathers might have helped Velociraptor keep cool. The

THEROPODS

Modern birds evolved from a group of dinosaurs called theropods. This group included large dinosaurs such as Tyrannosaurus as well as small dinosaurs such as Velociraptor. All theropods walked on two feet and ate meat. Many had similar traits to modern birds. Some, such as Velociraptor, even had a wishbone.

Like modern birds, Velociraptor made nests for its eggs.

feathers could have kept the dinosaur's body temperature low. Velociraptor could have used its feathers to protect its eggs from the hot sun as well.

CHAPTER 3

GOBI DESERT DAY

Velociraptor lived approximately 70 million years ago during the Late Cretaceous period. At this time, seas on Earth were warm and filled with **ammonites**. Ferns and trees covered the land. Flowers, mammals, and birds started to appear.

The area where Velociraptor lived was similar to the savanna in modern Africa.

Most of the planet had humid breezes. But Velociraptor lived in the Gobi Desert. Survival there was difficult. Sand stretched for more than 1,000 miles (1,600 km). The temperature was blistering hot during the day. At night, it was icy cold.

PACK HUNTERS

Some scientists think Velociraptor hunted alone. But most scientists believe Velociraptor gathered in packs to hunt. Closely related dinosaurs such as Deinonychus and Dromaeosaurus were also pack hunters. A group of Velociraptors could take down many kinds of prey. Their sharp teeth, dagger-like claws, and fast speeds would have made them hard to escape from.

A group of Velociraptors fights off a Tarbosaurus.

Velociraptor was most active after dark. At night, it prowled for food. Other predators such as Tarbosaurus sometimes attacked Velociraptor.

But even large dinosaurs could not have taken down a Velociraptor without a fight.

Velociraptor's diet likely included small reptiles and mammals. It may have eaten insects as well. It even hunted other dinosaurs. Most of these dinosaurs would have been small. But some were larger than Velociraptor.

In 1971, scientists discovered an amazing fossil in Mongolia. The desert sand had preserved the skeletons of two fighting dinosaurs. A Velociraptor had its claw jabbed into a Protoceratops's neck. This dinosaur had its tough beak clamped onto the Velociraptor's arm. Scientists think the dinosaurs killed each other and

The "Fighting Dinosaurs" fossil is on display in Ulaanbaatar, Mongolia.

stayed tangled. Then they were covered by a sudden sand storm.

This fossil was later named "Fighting Dinosaurs." It provided evidence that Velociraptor hunted Protoceratops. These parrot-beaked dinosaurs were bigger than Velociraptor. But Velociraptor was a good hunter. Herds of sleeping Protoceratops would have been an easy target.

CHAPTER 4

CRETACEOUS CRASH

Approximately 65 million years ago, a meteor crashed into Earth. Most scientists think this meteor is the reason that Velociraptor and other dinosaurs died out. The meteor caused earthquakes to rip apart the ground. Volcanoes spewed out hot lava. Winds spread wildfires, and dust blocked out the sun.

Velociraptor went extinct at the end of the Cretaceous period.

Darkness was everywhere. Without any vegetation left to eat, herbivores died first. Carnivores disappeared not long after.

Scientists still have questions about Velociraptor. They do not know what color it was. They do not have a good estimate for how much it weighed, either.

DISASTER EVIDENCE

The best proof of the meteor crash is a huge crater near Mexico. Called the Chicxulub crater, this huge hole is in the waters near the city of Cancun. Oil workers found it in 1978. Jumbled-up rock layers in Texas and the Caribbean Sea also indicate that something destructive happened at the end of the Cretaceous period.

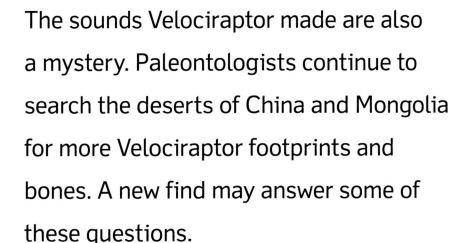

Museums also study current finds to reveal more about how Velociraptor moved and ate.

The sounds Velociraptor made are also a mystery. Paleontologists continue to search the deserts of China and Mongolia for more Velociraptor footprints and bones. A new find may answer some of these questions.

FOCUS ON
VELOCIRAPTOR

Write your answers on a separate piece of paper.

1. Write a sentence describing why Velociraptor was a good hunter.

2. If you were a dinosaur, would you rather be a giant herbivore or a small carnivore? What would be the advantages of each?

3. Velociraptor was about the size of what animal?

> **A.** a pigeon
> **B.** a turkey
> **C.** a sheep

4. Why do scientists think Velociraptor was smarter than other dinosaurs?

> **A.** Its relatively large brain would have allowed for more complex thinking.
> **B.** Its hunting strategies were more complicated and effective.
> **C.** Its social interactions suggest that it made specific choices and plans.

Answer key on page 32.

GLOSSARY

ammonites
Squid-like creatures that lived in spiral shells.

casts
Copies of fossils made by pouring plaster into a mold to give it the same shape as the original fossil.

evolved
Changed slowly over time, often becoming more complex.

excavated
Removed something from the ground by digging.

paleontologists
Scientists who study the ancient past and the fossil remains of ancient living things.

predator
An animal that hunts other animals for food.

prehistoric
From a very long time ago, before history was written down.

sockets
Holes or hollow areas that hold something.

species
A group of animals or plants that are similar.

TO LEARN MORE

BOOKS

Peterson, Sheryl. *Velociraptor*. Mankato, MN: Creative Education, 2010.

Thimmesh, Catherine. *Scaly Spotted Feathered Frilled: How Do We Know What Dinosaurs Really Looked Like?* Boston: Houghton Mifflin Harcourt, 2013.

West, David. *Velociraptor and Other Raptors and Small Carnivores*. New York: Gareth Stevens Publishing, 2011.

NOTE TO EDUCATORS

Visit **www.focusreaders.com** to find lesson plans, activities, links, and other resources related to this title.

INDEX

Answer Key: 1. Answers will vary; **2.** Answers will vary; **3.** B; **4.** A